The Nonnets

FIRST EDITION

The production of this book was made possible through the generous assistance
of the Canada Council for the Arts and the Ontario Arts Council. Book*hug also
acknowledges the support of the Government of Canada through the Canada Book
Fund and the Government of Ontario through the Ontario Book Publishing Tax
Credit and the Ontario Book Fund.

ONTARIO ARTS COUNCIL
CONSEIL DES ARTS DE L'ONTARIO
an Ontario government agency
un organisme du gouvernement de l'Ontario

Book*hug acknowledges the land on which it operates. For thousands of years
it has been the traditional land of the Huron-Wendat, the Seneca, and most recently,
the Mississaugas of the Credit River. Today, this meeting place is still the home
to many Indigenous people from across Turtle Island, and we are grateful to
have the opportunity to work on this land.

Library and Archives Canada Cataloguing in Publication

Giovannone, Aaron, 1979–, author
The nonnets / Aaron Giovannone.

Poems. Issued in print and electronic formats.
ISBN 978-1-77166-406-6 (softcover)
ISBN 978-1-77166-407-3 (HTML)
ISBN 978-1-77166-408-0 (PDF)
ISBN 978-1-77166-409-7 (Kindle)

I. Title.

PS8613.I68N66 2018   C811'.6   C2018-900814-8
                                             C2018-900815-6

PRINTED IN CANADA

The Nonnets

AARON GIOVANNONE

Book*hug
2018

I FEEL CLOSER to you

at the train crossing.

Cars line up, puff exhaust, annoyed

while faces in the train glide by.

Some notice me

and I wonder about them a centisecond each.

They seem extraordinary

but I don't have to talk to them.

Reader, you seem extraordinary.

TALKING TO HUMANS seems crazy.

I lean on the wall at a party

with nothing but whimsy, whimsy.

I am part of something here.

I nibble on SunChips.

Now they're part of me, and part of this.

My laptop's in my backpack by the door.

What a gift you've given us

whisper the robbers of laptops.

I LOOK UP what *nonplussed* means.

Dictionary.com pronounces it for me.

No, I won't do a robot voice for you

unless you ask nicely.

Holly22 phishes for my Visa number.

She's a Twitter bot, not a real girl.

Reader! Speak to me, are you there?

Are you also nonplussed?

A human's writing this, I swear.

LOVE DESTROYS DOUBLY

like smoking while sunbathing.

We stroll into each moment like

into a dark pub from the light

before Transitions lenses adjust.

Are those people whispering about us?

I'm getting to know you, so I say

my deepest fears are growing old

poor, and insane. But alone is okay.

WE LIE ON the trampoline, done

jumping, as the springs creak to a halt.

Under the stars, we connect the dots

in a philosophy that's only sprawling

interconnections. Raised Catholic, I confess

I want to be a different person.

I want to say the *h* in *white*

with extra aspiration—*whhhite*

like they do in New England.

A TEXT FROM you, with whom

my heart bounced higher.

I'll cite your message in MLA format.

In Cambridge

—Cambridge, Ontario, relax—

I'll disembark the Greyhound.

Dear CEO of Greyhound

the spider crawling across my headrest

is a symbol of your service.

TO HUG, WE spread our arms out like wings.

I like you laughing

and thinking I'm interesting.

The bucket of mop water

in the washroom of this bus terminal

is the worst place on Earth.

A pile of abandoned drug money

in a locker in this bus terminal

is the best place on Earth.

AT GOODWILL, WE pick through a bin of collectible pins.

I pin on this pin, you pin on that pin.

Every pin's a hypothetical situation.

You pull a rough wool sweater from the rack.

No one would hug me in that

which isn't a great situation.

Walking to the car, I'm already sad.

A crumpled bag of Dad's brand cookies

on the concrete really is my dad's.

A SNAP RATTLES on my Italian jacket.

It's not important it's Italian.

I just thought I'd mention it.

My hat says BMW.

I don't own a BMW

but I own this hat.

Oh, that's my phone, one minute.

The call's coming from inside your jacket!

Another pocket dial.

ON THE TRAIN at four p.m.

we close our eyes against the sun.

Well, not everyone.

A woman cries into her cellphone.

The clouds don't know they're clichés

but that's not why she's crying.

Reader, you double my joy

divide my sorrow in half.

That's relationship math.

ONE DECLARES WHAT kind of man one is

when she sits one down for bad news.

One feels one's face—it doesn't move.

I sense eternity around me, Calvin Klein's Eternity

when I spray from the bottle

I've had since I was twenty.

I float in sunlight, then starlight.

Oops, there's the sunlight again.

Oops, my equilibrium.

THE ANESTHESIOLOGIST TOUCHED my hand.

It'll be okay, she said.

I closed my eyes

then opened them.

The anesthesiologist's an excellent friend

I'll never see again.

Then Marc drove me home

in a Mitsubishi.

Then Netflix and oxycodone.

I UNWRAP A Kit Kat from the Mac's

step and chew in time

then buy another at the next Mac's I pass.

It's not my fault

there are too many Mac's in this neighbourhood.

I know I'm in a bad mood

when strangers apologize to me

but, Reader, I should apologize to you.

Really, I should!

I DON'T DRINK Big Gulps

because of the calories.

At least, I don't drink them publicly.

At the Art Gallery of Ontario

I exit the elevator at the wrong floor.

A waiter hands me stemware.

I'm in the Portuguese Wine Club now!

Tasting vinho verde and port

I could spit out, but don't.

CALCULATING, I SQUEEZE an unripe avocado.

I have crunched the numbers

and the celery stalks.

Is this what my mother wanted for me

to be squishy on the inside

an unstable admixture?

Soon I'll be old enough to believe

the music at Safeway is okay.

Even if I am wise, I will be wrong.

THE WOMAN AT the till

is the sister of a woman I've met.

I ask, *How are you? Your sister?*

But I'll never really know.

How are you, Reader?

I, too, sit hermetically sealed

with a book in my mom's condo.

The light seems weird in here.

Does the light seem weird to you?

AT SAFEWAY, THEY play

the Jackson 5's "ABC" (an okay song)

and a boy falsettos to a girl

while other shoppers smile.

Eloquence is heard, poetry overheard.

That's John Stuart Mill.

A butterfly flutters by.

That's my grandmother's soul.

If you laughed at that, you're dead inside.

I SHOW MOM how to use Netflix.

I'm the coolest person

my mom hangs out with.

My weakening belief in friendship

means you'll talk shit when I'm not around

like we do about you.

Saying it here isn't saying it for real.

I'm asleep in a rose garden—why not?

I mount a unicorn and ride off.

CHRIS MADE FUN of me

for carrying an umbrella in this city.

Now who's laughing.

At home, a bed awaits.

For the third time today

I think about it.

My sneakers squeak on slick, wooden steps.

If I lie down in damp clothes

will I nap? Let's see.

WHEN GREENPEACE CANVASSERS stop me

I say, *I'm late for a meeting.*

This is the meeting.

Just to be here's amazing.

I'd like to thank the many people

who believed in me.

That was your first mistake.

A silver maple with twinkling leaves.

Just kidding. There's no tree.

AT A BACKYARD firepit

a spark burns a hole in my jacket.

I'd buy a new one, but I can't.

We drink, smoke, and talk

while developers plan to knock

the whole block down for condos

including this spot.

We stare at the fire

while under us, the ground shifts.

WOODSMOKE FROM FOREST fires

wafts through the city.

It creeps up on me.

Far away, you

sip coffee with a book.

I hope it's this book.

With old friends in a living room

I touch a teacup to my lips

imagining you.

THE NEIGHBOURHOOD SMELLS of lilacs

but how could I be so naive?

When the evacuation was announced on CBC

I stuffed the cupboards with books

piled them on top of the fridge.

I own very little, Reader.

Would you take me with you in a flood?

When I'm gone, you'll see things differently.

Am I gone yet?

I WON'T GO out drinking in a cowboy hat.

I might stay home drinking in a cowboy hat.

I declined a Stampede party because I feel vulnerable.

Wait—now I'm triumphant

on McHugh Bluff, gazing upon the city

and the snow-capped mountains.

Wait—now I'm vulnerable again

knee-deep in a flooded basement.

Soon the rent will rise above my head.

AT TWILIGHT, TEENS dash across the country road

with a gust of chinook.

In case you don't know

the *chinook* is a warm, violent wind

that rattles southern Alberta

and *twilight* is symbolic of the end.

Clouds with lit undercarriages

mingle with the Rockies

so you can't distinguish them.

I'VE LEARNED PARSIMONY

from the farmers in my family

but I'm not special.

Off the highway, I pee in a poplar grove.

I see the empty pasture

and hoofprints in the snow.

The plow in the rear-view mirror shoots sparks.

With the lanes already clear

sparks seem to be the point.

WHAT IS LOVE? asks he

who might not love anything.

Fine, it's me asking.

Is love a feeling

for cheesecake topping?

It makes life impossible.

The couple sharing earbuds

their cheeks nearly touching

aren't listening.

OKAY. TIME TO get serious.

I am very serious: look at this

python-fat cable I lock my bicycle with.

It's a sleepy afternoon

but I won't lie on the bench

because I'll look homeless.

The best thing today

was a jpeg of a Wu-Tang Clan latte.

The real latte I drank didn't even rank.

I SLEPT LATE because it was still dark.

I pause, look up from my book.

Today I feel okay away from *you*

an abstraction like *future value*.

I wear white sneakers with black jeans

because I've given up a little.

At the café, a teenage boy

reads the Bible.

I wonder how it's going.

A SUNSHINE-YELLOW hoodie.

If I'm happy

am I happy with everything?

A smile for yoga class

and for you.

We perfect our minds and bodies.

Live in a dream, yoga teacher intones.

My dream's

to live in a poem.

YOU HAUL A duffle bag stuffed with gym clothes

or bricks of cocaine.

Look, I don't know what's in your duffle bag.

I can't be the only one who's afraid.

Is that footsteps in the alley

or blood pumping in my ears?

Don't believe it if my nose bleeds.

It's a trick for sympathy

I learned from *Rocky*.

IT'S HARD TO care

in the same yellow hoodie as yesterday

at the bar in a bowling alley

where everyone's a piece of shit

like me. I watch

an eleven-year-old drink coffee.

On Facebook, you seem to think

you're having fun, but you're not.

Not without me, you're not.

IT'S FREEZING ON the plane

so I don't fear

severe heat warnings on Earth.

On the news, a desperate man

thrusts his head into a fountain.

I zip my hoodie up.

A cape enfolds us both.

O, to disappear

like breath on a window.

WALKING IN FLORENCE alone makes me strong.

I mount steps with grass between the stones

around corners, encounter pure awe.

The Duomo bounces in my vision when I walk

like I'm a juggernaut

who approaches beauty, feeling ugly.

Above me, the dark cupola

could be anything.

Heavy, but empty.

BOOTED BY THE goalie, the ball soars.

Drunk fans drain red plastic cups.

Our pleasure waiting for the ball to drop.

Sandro, our striker, leaps

kicks the other team's defender.

Fireworks.

The abbey is just beyond, in fog.

I feel wronged because it's rained so much.

My umbrella a halo.

IT'S RAINING IN Casamari

an eleventh-century abbey with a library.

A monk rolls a cigarette, looks up, and smiles.

Italians are cool.

I wander the yard with my hood up

my hands clasped behind me.

It's great being a monk

so long as I can leave whenever I want.

I'll snap a selfie in the cemetery.

A LIT CIGARETTE in a graveyard.

I don't think

I'm allowed to smoke here

but no one says so

because everyone is dead.

I puff my cheeks out for that photo.

Sometimes a cigar is just a cigar

but sometimes it's a phallus

especially to you guys.

PILLARS CARVED A millennium ago.

I put my hand on the cold stone

to conjure the artisans' thoughts.

Nope, nothing.

A priest slouches in a pew

in the middle of the marble expanse.

It's the centre of a universe

I don't believe in

but I marvel at the stained glass.

HAVE YOU EVER sat in a pew

when light breaks through

the stained glass, and you glow too?

Wish you were here. Actually, no.

It seemed like something I should say.

I'd rather be alone. Suddenly—

suddenly is rarely used well—

an older me exists, maybe

when you read this.

THEY SAY, *LA bara*, the casket

when they mean

the dead person who's in it.

Returned home from the funeral

Zia delivers a Dixie plate

tented in foil.

I lift it, spangling, to reveal

angel food cake!

I am translated.

ARRIVEDERCI ROMA: GOOD Buy Roma

the airport duty-free.

Get it? It took me a minute.

The escalator accelerates

when I step on it.

Calm in controlled air quality.

An elderly man in the window seat

reaches, trembling, across me.

I pass his drink to him.

LYNN AND I watched *Troy*

sitting in the beat-up seats

of Town Cinemas, now closed.

Mom phones about the rainbow.

At the vet's, I step outside

to look at the sky.

At home, I open the cage.

Tuppens the cat slinks out

slips under the bed.

AT THE HOSPITAL cafeteria

I fumbled

with the coffee machine.

A doctor in line behind me

grabbed my cup

and filled it. She said

It takes a degree from MIT

to work this coffee machine.

That's how she diagnosed me.

BREAKFAST, MY LAST inheritance.

My grandpa left me money.

I buy a cinnamon bun

that tumbles in my belly.

The underworld.

It's destroying me on the inside.

Bagga—that's what we called him.

I unlock my apartment

and step inside an Ikea catalogue.

AT A CAFÉ for comedy.

Cut to a body

shrouded for cremation.

The oven door opens.

Laughter rises.

The body enters, exits ashes.

At Pita Pit, I'm pointing

at toppings, and coughing

from the same infection.

ONCE, I WAS afraid of sabre-toothed tigers.

Now it's a hungry cat in the morning

gnawing toes through blankets. Get off me.

I'm quick beside the mountains

but slow beside investment capital.

My feeling is a fridge buzzing.

I slept on Jesse's couch after the party.

His fridge of vegan leftovers looks great.

My fridge (if you come over, you'll see) is a disgrace.

AT THE KALAMATA grocery

the clerk seems sad tonight.

I buy Greek yogurt (but not cigarettes, I resist)

then hop on my bike.

It's colder along the river.

I duck the Tenth Street bridge, pedal like mad

toward a couple paused under a lamp.

High five? the girl asks.

I slap her palm as I pass.

IT SEEMED THERE would never be a time

Obama wasn't president.

Now look.

A Canadian prime minister chokes up

delivering an address

at a soldier's funeral

when he says the phrase *the children*.

I know that trick.

We think of our own.

CHOCOLATE ALMONDS PILFERED

from bulk bins, but no one sees.

I confess

because this is confessional poetry.

Open up, it's the police—

I mean, room service.

Quick, flip the mattress

to block the door!

I'll grab the Bible from the drawer.

THE USED BOOK shop

sells beach reading

for tourists and the elderly.

Sunlight is bad for screens.

I'm prepared to admit

this is why I still need books.

At Black Lake, my grandmother

sat with a novel, scanning

the surface, for us swimming.

I'M NOT A kid, but I act like one.

When the waves in the wave pool stop

I climb out, towel off, grow up.

How much do I owe the bank? $34,000.

That's not so bad.

The waves curl above my head—

the lights flicker, we all look up.

Reader, is it true

a disaster would bring us together?

AT HOUR FIVE of working at home

the belt comes off with a bullwhip flourish.

Too early for peejays—

it's the right time for *pre*-jays.

The cat watches, tail swooshing.

Okay, tough guy, tell me

what's the point of Earl Grey tea

without tons of milk and honey?

There is no point, stop arguing.

I ordered Chinese for two

so they wouldn't know I ate alone.

I ate Chinese for two.

My phone blinks *hey man, hey man.*

All my passwords

are happyCAT31.

I text and drive.

Do you say *HYundai* or *HyUNdai?*

Anyway, I'm about to die in mine.

I REGRET NOT wearing my bathrobe enough.

It's a great bathrobe.

That's not my only regret.

At seventeen, I loved *Good Will Hunting*.

I rhapsodized about it driving Cathy home.

Cathy, I'm sorry.

This is embarrassing

like the Rammstein CD

someone forgot in the rental car.

SHE SAID, *YOU snore like a wharfie.*

I hadn't heard that expression before.

She explained, *A wharfie is a stevedore.*

I nodded blankly.

The pinot grigio she poured into my glass

I poured into my mouth

then she poured some more.

I sleep, snore, and dream

yawn, turn on the espresso machine.

A MYSTERIOUS SMELL of coffee.

Bathrobed, sleepy, you pad toward the kitchen

halt before the vision.

Your son, so handsome in uniform

has returned from the war.

He touches a mug of Folgers to his lips.

But wait—why Folgers?

That's when you know it isn't your son.

It's that commercial for Folgers from 1991.

WITHOUT YOU, I am the man

at the next table

talking to himself.

Now he's talking to me. Help.

I peeled a banana

to make you a lily.

Don't leave me

alone in the park

thinking about beauty.

MY PHONE'S GPS paused at a winery

for seventy minutes.

My credit card was charged

ninety-six dollars.

I know how this looks.

Yes, I adore champagne

but I was buying gifts that day.

I don't see why not wasn't a lie.

I didn't see why not.

ZOOMING SEMIS ROCK my car

on the highway's shoulder.

Hazards flash in a gallery of pine.

Is anyone else here afraid of bears

or of that rusted blue pickup

parked at the edge of the woods?

Because we're alive, we're growing

a moustache, at least its wispy beginnings.

Dead, we will be too.

WILD HORSES GRAZE the canal bank.

They've escaped

but where to?

A long-haired couple in their forties

point at listings

in a real estate office window

then roll away on skateboards.

I wonder, Reader, if we should do that.

The answer is no.

I SANG OUT loud

in the underground parking garage

because I lived beyond want.

Turning the corner, I was startled

by Elenore, our neighbour

hunched over her walker.

Just one set of footprints in the sand

in an inspirational poem.

We're really not alone.

HERE'S YOUR NEGATIVE review of my life:

happiness comes in cartons of Häagan-Dazs

and sadness comes in cartons of Häagan-Dazs.

You have no way of knowing if I'm really

unshaven, shirtless, in sweatpants tonight

but you might as well imagine it.

Reader, let's take this broken relationship

to the relation-*shop*—I tried, I'm sorry.

Avoiding eye contact, I back away slowly.

CROSSING THE CROWDED Peace Bridge on foot

with walkers, joggers, cyclists

the Bow River lunging

I caught three words of a conversation.

Non abbiamo noi—we don't have, in Italian.

I couldn't tell who said it

but I looked at each face, dear to me now.

Like happiness and sadness

what carried me over the river was temporary.

Acknowledgements

Thank you, early readers and audiences, especially Palmer Olson and Jake "PSB" Kennedy.

Thank you, Mom.

Thank you, Canada Council for the Arts, British Columbia Arts Council, Okanagan College, Sage Hill Writing Centre, and Banff Centre for Arts and Creativity.

Thank you, Karen Solie, for your editorial advice.

Thank you, Shawn Mankowske, for your painting.

Thank you, Hazel Millar and Jay MillAr, and everyone at Book*hug.

And thank you, Naomi, my Dearest Reader.

About the Author

Aaron Giovannone's poems have been published widely in journals across Canada and the US, and his nonfiction has appeared or is forthcoming in *The Walrus*, *Brick*, and *Vice*. Originally from St. Catharines, Ontario, Aaron has a Ph.D. in English Literature and Creative Writing from the University of Calgary and has lived in Italy, including a year as a visiting scholar at the University of Siena. He is the author of a previous collection of poetry titled *The Loneliness Machine*. Aaron splits his time between Calgary and the Okanagan Valley, where he teaches literature and writing at Okanagan College.

Colophon

Manufactured as the first edition of *The Nonnets*
in the spring of 2018 by Book*hug.

Distributed in Canada by the Literary Press Group: lpg.ca

Distributed in the United States by Small Press
Distribution: spdbooks.org

Shop online at bookthug.ca

BOOK
PRODUCTION
WAR ECONOMY
STANDARD

Edited for the press by Karen Solie
Copy edited by Stuart Ross
Type + design by Tree Abraham